ANTWERP
VACATION GUIDE
2023

The Essential and Ultimate Guide to Antwerp's Hotels, Cuisines, Shopping Tips, Insider's Tips, Top Attractions, History, and Culture

ALFRED FLORES

Copyright © 2023, Alfred Flores

All rights reserved. No part of this publication may be reproduced, distributed, or transmitted in any form or by any means, including photocopying, recording, or other electronic or mechanical methods, without the prior written permission of the publisher, except in the case of brief quotations embodied in critical reviews and certain other noncommercial uses permitted by copyright law.

TABLE OF CONTENTS

INTRODUCTION

CHAPTER ONE:

Getting to Know Antwerp

   Geographical Overview

   Climate and Weather

   History and Culture

   Festivals and Events

CHAPTER TWO:

Planning Your Trip to Antwerp

   Best Time to Visit Antwerp

   Visa and Travel Requirements

   How to Get There

   Getting Around

   Accommodation Options

   Travel Insurance

CHAPTER THREE:

Exploring Antwerp's Neighborhoods

Old Town (Historic Center)

Zurenborg

Eilandje

South Antwerp (Het Zuid)

Diamond District

CHAPTER FOUR:

Top Attractions in Antwerp

Antwerp Cathedral (Onze-Lieve-Vrouwekathedraal)

Rubenshuis (Rubens House)

MAS (Museum aan de Stroom)

Museum Plantin-Moretus

Antwerp Zoo

CHAPTER FIVE:

Hidden Gems of Antwerp

Middelheim Museum and Sculpture Park

Vlaeykensgang - The Hidden Alleyway

De Koninck Brewery

Carolus Borromeus Church

St. Anna's Tunnel (Sint-Anna Voetgangerstunnel)

CHAPTER SIX: Antwerp's Cultural Scene
- Museums and Art Galleries
- Theaters and Performing Arts
- Music and Concerts
- Cultural Festivals and Events
- Diamond District Tours

CHAPTER SEVEN:
Antwerp's Culinary Delights
- Traditional Belgian Cuisine
- Flemish Specialties and Beer
- International Dining Options
- Local Food Markets
- Frites and Waffles

CHAPTER EIGHT:
Shopping in Antwerp
- Fashion and Design District

    Antwerp's Fashion Boutiques

    Antiques and Vintage Shops

    Souvenirs and Gifts

    Chocolate and Confectionery

CHAPTER NINE:

Nightlife in Antwerp

    Bars and Pubs

    Trendy Nightclubs

    Live Music Venues

    Jazz Bars and Cafés

    Cultural Evenings

CHAPTER TEN:

Outdoor Adventures near Antwerp

    Parks and Green Spaces

    Cycling and Biking Routes

    Boat Tours and Cruises

    Day Trips to Surrounding Towns

    Sports and Recreation

CHAPTER ELEVEN:

Unraveling Antwerp's History

  Antwerp's Golden Age

  The Diamond Trade Legacy

  World War II and Its Impact

  Architectural Heritage

  Art and Cultural Heritage

CHAPTER TWELVE:

Insider's Tips for a Memorable Antwerp Vacation

  Local Etiquette and Customs

  Money-Saving Tips

  Off-the-Beaten-Path Spots

  Safety Precautions

CHAPTER THIRTEEN:

Appendix

  30 Useful Phrases in Dutch and Pronunciation Guide

  Currency Conversion Chart

  Packing List for Antwerp

MAP OF ANTWERP

INTRODUCTION

Welcome to Antwerp, Belgium's dynamic and alluring city! You are in for an amazing experience in this stunning Belgian city, regardless of whether you are an experienced tourist or a first-time visitor. A real treasure, Antwerp has a vibrant cultural scene, a long history, and a special fusion of tradition and contemporary. Antwerp, a bustling port city on the banks of the River Scheldt, has long been a crossroads of various cultures and a center of world trade.

Why Go to Antwerp?
Antwerp should be at the top of your list of places to visit. Among the numerous compelling

reasons to visit this extraordinary city, the following are just a few:

- Cultural Heritage: Antwerp's history, which dates back to the Roman era, is clearly visible across the entire city. You will be in awe of Antwerp's rich cultural legacy, which includes magnificent Renaissance works and breathtaking medieval structures like the Cathedral of Our Lady and the city hall.

- Artistic Marvels: Being the birthplace of famed painter Peter Paul Rubens, Antwerp has a strong tie to the art world. Now a museum honoring his life and work, the Rubenshuis was once his home and studio. The Royal Museum of Fine Arts, which houses a noteworthy collection of

Belgian and Flemish works of art, is another place that art lovers will enjoy.

- Fashion and Shopping: Known as one of the world's fashion capitals, Antwerp is a forward-thinking city when it comes to fashion and shopping. Fashionistas and shoppers will find plenty of chic shops, upscale clothing stores, and cutting-edge designer outlets on the streets.

- Culinary Delights: Belgian cuisine is renowned around the world, and Antwerp is no exception. Enjoy the city's rich eating scene, which offers everything from traditional Belgian dishes to international culinary pleasures, or indulge in scrumptious chocolates, waffles, and mussels.

- Diamond District: Often referred to as the "Diamond Capital of the World," Antwerp's Diamond District is a must-see destination for anybody with an interest in priceless gemstones. Admire exquisite jewelry or possibly buy a shining memento to treasure always.

How to Use This Guide

The goal of this guide is to make the most of your time in Antwerp. We have put together a thorough resource to make your stay unforgettable, whether you're planning a quick weekend escape or a longer trip. Here's how to navigate this guide:

- Attractions and Sightseeing: Discover the greatest attractions, museums, and landmarks that characterize Antwerp's charm and personality.

- Activities and Entertainment: There are a ton of things to do to keep you entertained, from cultural events to leisure activities.

- Dining and Nightlife: Take a look at Antwerp's many dining options and exciting nightlife.

- Practical Information: Discover helpful hints on how to get around the city easily, as well as details on the weather, regional customs, and other pertinent topics.
- Accommodation: Find the perfect place to stay, whether you prefer luxury hotels, cozy bed-and-breakfasts, or budget-friendly hostels.

Antwerp: Quick Facts and Statistics

- Location: Flanders, a region in northern Belgium, is home to Antwerp.

- Population: According to the most recent figures from 2021, Antwerp has a population of about 529,247, making it the most populous city in Belgium.

- Language: Although English is commonly spoken, especially in tourist areas, Dutch is Antwerp's official language.

- Currency: The Euro (EUR), like the rest of Belgium, is the official currency in Antwerp.

- Climate: Antwerp experiences warm summers and chilly winters because of its temperate coastal climate. The finest seasons to travel are spring and summer, when the climate is most agreeable.

- Transportation: It is simple to get around the city and visit its surroundings in Antwerp because of the city's effective public transit system, which includes trams, buses, and trains.

Immerse yourself in Antwerp's rich history, culture, and energetic environment as you explore the city's attractions. Whether you love art, history, food, or are just looking for a relaxing break, Antwerp is sure to capture your heart and leave you with priceless memories. So let's set out on this trip together and find all the hidden gems in Antwerp!

CHAPTER ONE:
Getting to Know Antwerp

Geographical Overview

In the northern part of Belgium, in the Flanders region, Antwerp, sometimes known as the "Diamond City," is a bustling and multicultural metropolis. It is located on the right bank of the River Scheldt, one of Europe's major waterways, which was essential to the city's growth into a thriving port and a hub of commerce. Due to its advantageous location close to the North Sea, Antwerp serves as a significant marine entryway to Europe.

The city is divided into a number of districts, each with its own distinctive personality and allure, and it has a total area of about 204 square kilometers (79 square miles). With gorgeous architecture, cobblestone streets, and charming squares, the ancient city center is a bustling bustle of activity. The nearby neighborhoods offer a blend of tradition and modernity along with hip stores, cultural centers, and parks.

Climate and Weather

The proximity of Antwerp to the North Sea has an impact on the city's mild maritime climate. Although there can be a lot of variation in the weather throughout the year, it typically has warm summers and cool winters. Here is a list of the seasons:

- Spring (March to May): Spring is a lovely season to travel to Antwerp since the city comes to life with beautiful flowers and comfortable weather. The range of daily highs and lows is between 10°C and 15°C (50°F and 59°F).

- Summer (June to August): Antwerp experiences pleasant to warm summers, with average highs of 18°C to 23°C (64°F to 73°F). Tourists frequently use this time to stroll across the city, take in outdoor events, and unwind in the parks.

- Autumn (September to November): Autumn is characterized by a change in weather and a colorful display of fall leaves. The range of daily highs and lows is between 10°C and 15°C (50°F and 59°F).

- Winter (December to February): The winters in Antwerp can be frigid, with typical highs of 2 to 6 degrees Celsius (36 to 43 degrees Fahrenheit).

Even if it doesn't snow often, the holidays give the city a mystical allure.

History and Culture

Antwerp has a fascinating past that goes all the way back to Roman times. It has gone through periods of economic success, artistic renaissance, and cultural influence over the years. Antwerp rose to prominence in the Hanseatic League and became one of Europe's most significant trading hubs during the Middle Ages. The city was able to develop into a center of Renaissance art and architecture thanks to the port's expansion and the wealth brought in by foreign trade.

Under the authority of the Habsburgs, Antwerp flourished as a significant commercial and

CHAPTER TWO:
Planning Your Trip to Antwerp

Best Time to Visit Antwerp

The ideal time of year to visit Antwerp is entirely dependent on your tastes and areas of interest. When choosing when to schedule your trip, take into account the following variables:

1. Spring (March to May): Spring is a lovely season to travel to Antwerp since the city comes to life with beautiful flowers and more comfortable weather. Exploring the city's parks and gardens as well as sightseeing are all highly recommended at this time of year.

2. Summer (June to August): With warm weather and a busy ambiance, summer is

Antwerp's busiest travel season. Festivals, outdoor activities, and relaxing on the city's numerous patios and cafes are all wonderful during this time. However, at this time, expect larger crowds and more expensive lodging.

3. Autumn (September to November): Autumn ushers in a period of colder temperatures as well as a vibrant display of fall foliage. Avoiding the busiest tourist seasons is a wonderful way to enjoy Antwerp's museums, galleries, and cultural events.

4. Winter (December to February): Antwerp is at its most tranquil during the winter, making it the perfect time to visit. Christmastime in the city is a time for festive markets and wintertime activities. Although it can get chilly, the environment is warm and welcoming.

Visa and Travel Requirements

Make sure you have the required travel documents and verify the visa requirements for your country of residency before you depart for Antwerp. Belgium is a part of the Schengen Area, which enables people from numerous nations to travel without a visa. You'll probably need a Schengen visa to enter Belgium if you're from a non-Schengen nation.

Visit the website of the Belgian embassy or consulate in your country to submit an application for a Schengen visa. Apply well in advance of the dates you intend to go, as the visa application procedure could take several weeks.

How to Get There

Due to its numerous international connections, Antwerp is simple to reach by air, train, or car.

1. By Air: Antwerp International Airport (ANR) is the city's primary international airport. It provides flights to a number of European destinations and is especially practical for visitors arriving from within Europe. To get to Antwerp, you can take a long-distance flight into either Brussels Airport (BRU) or Amsterdam Airport Schiphol (AMS), both of which offer great transportation connections.

2. By Train: Major European cities are well-connected by rail from Antwerp. You can take a fast train to Antwerp Central Station if you're coming from a nearby nation like the

Netherlands, France, Germany, or the United Kingdom.

3. By Road: The European road system connects Antwerp with its surrounding nations. If you prefer to travel by car, Antwerp is conveniently located close to places like Amsterdam, Brussels, Paris, and Cologne.

Getting Around

Since Antwerp is a small city, many of its attractions are close to one another. To move around the city, there are a number of different transportation choices, including:

1. Buses and Trams: De Lijn operates a large and effective bus and tram network in Antwerp. For both citizens and visitors, trams are a preferred

means of transportation since they make it simple to go around the city.

2. Bicycles: Antwerp is a bike-friendly city with dedicated cycling lanes and bike-sharing services. Renting a bicycle is a convenient way to explore the city at your own pace.

3. Metro: Antwerp has a small metro system, with four lines that cover the main areas of the city.

4. Taxis and Ride-Sharing: Uber and other ride-sharing services are both freely available in Antwerp.

Accommodation Options

Antwerp provides a variety of lodging choices to fit every need and preference. Here are a few instances:

1. Luxury Hotels: Antwerp features a number of luxury hotels that offer attractive accommodations, first-rate amenities, and top-notch service if you're seeking for a luxurious place to stay. Hotel Julien, Hotel De Witte Lelie, and Hotel Rubens-Grote Markt are a few examples.

2. Boutique Hotels: If you want a more distinctive and tailored experience, Antwerp's boutique hotels are a terrific option. These hotels frequently have chic decor, cozy surroundings,

and unique details. Hotel Banks, Hotel Matelote, and Hotel Pilar are a few examples.

3. Mid-Range Hotels: There are many mid-range hotels in Antwerp that provide cozy accommodations and high-quality extras without breaking the wallet. Examples include Hotel O Kathedral, Ibis Antwerpen Centrum, and Lindner Hotel & City Lounge Antwerpen.

4. Budget Accommodations: Travelers on a tight budget can locate inexpensive hostels and low-cost motels in Antwerp. Examples include The ASH, Yust Antwerp, and Antwerp Central Youth Hostel.

Zurenborg

An area known for its stunning and unique architecture is Zurenborg. It is a haven for lovers of architecture with a wide variety of magnificent Art Nouveau and Belle Époque structures. Each home on the Cogels-Osylei street features distinctive designs, elaborate facades, and minute details, making the street particularly well known for its architectural diversity.

In addition to its amazing architecture, Zurenborg is a bustling neighborhood with a variety of cafes, pubs, and restaurants. Locals frequently congregate at the Dageraadplaats area to socialize and partake in meals or beverages in a lively setting.

Eilandje

Eilandje, which means "Little Island," is a vibrant and quickly growing community near the Scheldt River. It was once a port region, but in recent years, major renovation has transformed it into a fashionable waterfront zone with a blend of the old and the new.

In Eilandje, the famed MAS (Museum aan de Stroom) dominates the landscape. This contemporary museum highlights Antwerp's nautical history and has a rooftop with panoramic views. Visitors can discover the history, variety, and international trade of the city.

Additionally, Eilandje is home to smart cafes, chic restaurants, and trendy bars. It's a great location for enjoying a leisurely stroll along the riverbank and seeing the modern buildings and scenery.

South Antwerp (Het Zuid)

Het Zuid, or South Antwerp, is a fashionable and creative district noted for its cutting-edge art galleries, posh shops, and thriving cultural environment. It's a center for creativity and a top destination for both locals and tourists.

One of the most notable attractions in Het Zuid is the Royal Museum of Fine Arts, also known as the KMSKA. It has a sizable collection of Belgian and Flemish artwork, including pieces by illustrious creators including Rubens, Van Dyck, and Ensor.

Het Zuid also has a ton of hip bars, quaint cafes, and fashionable eateries. It's a wonderful location for gastronomic indulgence, a night out, or just people-watching in one of the quaint squares.

Diamond District

The "Diamond Capital of the World" is Antwerp's Diamond District, which is a thriving area close to the Central Station and one of the greatest diamond trading hubs in the world, handling a sizeable amount of the world's rough and polished diamonds.

The Diamond District has a wide variety of jewelry stores where visitors may look around and view the gorgeous diamonds and other precious gemstones on show. Even if you don't intend to buy jewelry, it's fascinating to see the artistry and the diamond trade in action.

Additionally, the neighborhood offers a lively multinational atmosphere, with a variety of eateries and shops reflecting the city's cosmopolitan nature.

You can gain a well-rounded understanding of Antwerp's history, architecture, culture, and modern way of life by exploring these many areas. Every neighborhood in this enchanting Belgian city has its own distinctive attractions and atmosphere, making it possible for every visitor to discover something special to enjoy.

CHAPTER FOUR:
Top Attractions in Antwerp

An abundance of fascinating attractions are available for visitors to explore in Antwerp, a city steeped in history, culture, and the arts. These top five sights ought to be on every traveler's list:

Antwerp Cathedral (Onze-Lieve-Vrouwekathedraal)

One of Belgium's most outstanding Gothic cathedrals and a UNESCO World Heritage Site is the Antwerp Cathedral, also called the Cathedral of Our Lady. With a towering spire that is more than 123 meters (403 feet) tall, it dominates the skyline of the city. The cathedral's building process started in the 14th century and lasted for several decades.

The cathedral's interior is spectacular, with a stunning collection of artworks that includes works by renowned painter Peter Paul Rubens. Two significant features of the cathedral are Rubens' "The Elevation of the Cross" and "The Descent from the Cross."

Atop the tower, visitors may get a bird's-eye perspective over Antwerp and its surroundings. In addition to serving as a place of prayer, the Antwerp Cathedral is also a veritable museum of the city's extensive artistic legacy.

Rubenshuis (Rubens House)

The famed Flemish Baroque painter Peter Paul Rubens previously called the historic mansion The Rubenshuis, or Rubens House, his home and studio. This stunning structure provides a window into the acclaimed artist's life and creative legacy.

Visitors can tour Rubens' former residence, his studio, and a stunning garden inside the Rubenshuis. An excellent collection of his paintings, as well as pieces by his contemporaries and successors, are on display at the museum. Admire the sculptures, works of art, and vintage furnishings that adorn the spaces and offer an insight into the sumptuous way of life of the Baroque era.

The Rubenshuis is a must-see for anyone interested in art, history, or getting a glimpse into the life of one of the greatest artists in human history.

MAS (Museum aan de Stroom)

The Museum aan de Stroom, also referred to as MAS, is a stunning modern museum located in Antwerp's Eilandje neighborhood. The museum is devoted to displaying the maritime history, culture, and ties of the city.

The structure of the building itself is a work of art in architecture, with a distinctive spiraling pattern. Visitors can travel through Antwerp's past, present, and future within. The museum's extensive holdings include items from the fields of exploration, trade, and shipping.

The rooftop of the MAS, which provides expansive views of Antwerp's cityscape and the River Scheldt, is one of its best features. It's a fantastic location to take in stunning views of the city and its bustling port district.

Museum Plantin-Moretus

One of the oldest printing museums in the world is the Museum Plantin-Moretus, which is a UNESCO World Heritage Site. It is housed in the former home and printing facility of the Plantin-Moretus family, renowned Renaissance printers and publishers.

The museum offers insight into the history of printing and the craft of bookmaking through its enormous collection of printing presses, typefaces, manuscripts, and books. Visitors are welcome to tour the exquisitely restored 16th-century interiors, which include the family's residences, libraries, and offices.

One of the few remaining copies of the Gutenberg Bible is one of the rare books in the museum's collection. The Museum Plantin-Moretus is a fascinating location for history and book aficionados since it sheds light on the development of printing and how it affected the spread of knowledge.

Antwerp Zoo

One of the oldest and most well-known zoological parks in the world is the Antwerp Zoo, which opened its doors in 1843. It is close to Antwerp Central Station, spans a vast area, and offers visitors of all ages a fun and instructive experience.

More than 5,000 animals representing more than 950 species live in the zoo. The varied collection, which includes reptiles, aquatic life, and exotic mammals and birds, provides a fascinating look into the animal realm. In naturalistic habitats, visitors can view creatures like elephants, giraffes, lions, penguins, and many others.

Antwerp Zoo is a lovely spot to stroll about and unwind thanks to its lovely gardens and architectural elements. It is a fun-filled day of exploration and wonderment for everyone and is a family-friendly destination.

The greatest attractions in Antwerp appeal to a variety of interests, from nature and wildlife to art and history. Each location showcases the city's rich cultural history, originality, and vibrant personality, giving guests a really unforgettable and rewarding experience. Whatever your interests—art, history, or nature—Antwerp has something very special to offer.

CHAPTER FIVE:
Hidden Gems of Antwerp

Even while Antwerp's top attractions are well-known and attract a sizable number of tourists, the city still contains several undiscovered jewels that provide distinctive and enthralling experiences. Off the main road, these lesser-known locations offer a window into various facets of Antwerp's history, culture, and everyday life. Here are five undiscovered jewels just waiting to be found:

Middelheim Museum and Sculpture Park

In the southern section of Antwerp, the Middelheim Museum and Sculpture Park is a tranquil haven of art and nature. The park is one of the most significant open-air sculpture museums in Europe, measuring 30 hectares (74 acres) and housing an exceptional collection of modern and contemporary sculptures.

Due to the sculptures' dispersed location across the park, visitors may engage with and fully experience the artwork. While strolling through the beautiful vegetation, visitors may see works by well-known artists including Henry Moore, Auguste Rodin, and Rik Wouters, among others.

The Middelheim Museum features transient exhibits, art projects, and performances, which enhances its dynamic and constantly-evolving nature. It's the ideal location for nature lovers and art lovers to connect in a peaceful environment with creativity and beauty.

Vlaeykensgang - The Hidden Alleyway

In the center of Antwerp's Old Town, Vlaeykensgang, also referred to as the "hidden alleyway," is a well-kept secret. This small passageway provides a window into the city's past and dates back to the sixteenth century. Vlaeykensgang, which formerly housed shoemakers, artists, and craftspeople, has kept much of its genuine medieval beauty.

On Hoogstraat, there is a tiny opening between two buildings that leads to the alleyway. When you enter, the cobblestone walkways, old facades, and lantern-lit tunnels will take you back in time. A few restaurants and cafes have since moved into the secret passageway, creating a warm and inviting atmosphere for a meal or drink.

The hidden gem of Vlaeykensgang provides a peaceful retreat from the busy city streets and a window into Antwerp's extensive past.

De Koninck Brewery

Beer lovers should discover the De Koninck Brewery, also called the "Bolleke" brewery. This venerable brewery, which is close to the Berchem district, has been making the renowned "Bolleke" beer for more than a century.

De Koninck Brewery offers guided tours that provide guests an in-depth understanding of the craft of brewing beer. Discover the brewing procedure, the brewery's past, and the relevance of "Bolleke" to Antwerp's beer tradition.

Visitors can enjoy the various flavors of De Koninck's brews during the tour's tasting session. It's a wonderful chance to learn about Antwerp's beer history and sample some great regional brews.

Carolus Borromeus Church

The Carolus Borromeus Church is a hidden gem worth discovering for its distinctive architectural style and historical significance, even if Antwerp Cathedral frequently steals the show. This 1621-completed Baroque church is devoted to Saint Charles Borromeo.

Beautiful Baroque decorations adorn the church's front, while its interior is filled with elaborate altars, decorations, and artwork. The exquisite Peter Paul Rubens ceiling paintings further enhance the church's aesthetic beauty.

Compared to the busy Antwerp Cathedral, Carolus Borromeus Church offers a calmer and more personal experience, making it a good place to ponder and admire Baroque art and architecture.

St. Anna's Tunnel (Sint-Anna Voetgangerstunnel)

The pedestrian tunnel, also known as St. Anna's Tunnel, connects the right and left sides of the River Scheldt and is a well-kept secret. The tunnel, built in the 1930s, allows bicyclists and pedestrians to cross the river without obstructing boat traffic.

The fact that there are old wooden escalators on both sides of the river leading to this tunnel gives it a special quality. You enter a vintage-style time capsule as you descend into the tube. The tiled walls, vintage lighting, and nostalgic ambiance of the tunnel make for an unforgettable experience.

You'll be in a new district of Antwerp as you cross over, giving you the chance to explore the less popular parts of the city.

These lesser-known sites in Antwerp provide a fascinating counterpoint to the city's well-known landmarks. They provide you the chance to learn more about lesser-known facets of Antwerp's history, art, culture, and way of life, enhancing and rewarding your trip to the city.

CHAPTER SIX:
Antwerp's Cultural Scene

The city of Antwerp is thriving on its culture, originality, and artistic expression. World-class museums and art galleries, as well as exciting theaters, musical performances, and cultural festivals, are just a few of the experiences available in this city's thriving cultural scene. Here is a detailed analysis of Antwerp's rich cultural offerings:

Museums and Art Galleries

The outstanding array of museums and galleries in Antwerp appeals to a variety of aesthetic preferences and interests. Among the cultural sites that are a must-see are:

1. Royal Museum of Fine Arts (KMSKA): The Royal Museum of Fine Arts is home to a remarkable collection of artwork by Belgian and Flemish artists, including pieces by James Ensor, Anthony van Dyck, and Peter Paul Rubens.

2. Museum aan de Stroom (MAS): Located in the Eilandje district, MAS is a contemporary museum focusing on Antwerp's maritime history, global connections, and cultural heritage.

3. Museum Plantin-Moretus: As one of the oldest printing museums in the world, this UNESCO World Heritage Site showcases the history of printing and bookmaking, along with an extensive collection of rare books and manuscripts.

symphonic concerts and other classical activities for fans of classical music.

Music and Concerts

The music scene in Antwerp is thriving and diverse, providing access to a variety of musical styles. You can catch local and international talent at the city's many concert halls, clubs, and live music pubs. Some popular music venues include:

1. Sportpaleis: One of Europe's largest indoor performance venues, Sportpaleis often holds significant musical events with top worldwide performers.

2. Trix: A buzzing music venue that features a variety of rock, indie, and alternative music as well as holding events for upcoming musicians.

3. Het Bos: With a concentration on experimental and underground music, this multipurpose venue presents concerts, performances, and cultural events.

Cultural Festivals and Events

The cultural calendar of Antwerp is jam-packed with celebrations of art, music, dance, film, and other forms of expression. Popular cultural festivals include the following:

1. Antwerp Art Weekend: An annual celebration of modern art, Antwerp Art Weekend features exhibitions, performances, and art installations all around the city.

2. Antwerp Pride: Antwerp Pride is a celebration of diversity and equality for LGBTQ+ people

that includes parades, parties, and cultural activities.

3. Bollekesfeest: A three-day celebration of Antwerp's traditions, gastronomy, and culture featuring lots of regional fare, music, and entertainment.

4. Jazz Middelheim: Top jazz musicians from all over the world come together for the annual Jazz Middelheim event, which takes place in Middelheim Park.

Diamond District Tours

There are guided excursions available to explore this distinctive area of the city, and the Diamond District of Antwerp provides intriguing insights into the world of diamonds. These tours provide an insight of the history, craftsmanship, and trade of the diamond business by taking tourists through diamond workshops, showrooms, and even the Diamond Exchange.

There is always something exciting and enriching to explore in Antwerp, regardless of your interests in art, music, theater, or cultural events. The city is a dynamic center of artistic expression and a delight for culture fans from all over the world because of its creative energy and numerous cultural offerings.

CHAPTER SEVEN:
Antwerp's Culinary Delights

Antwerp is a culinary paradise that offers a diverse selection of tastes and sensations to entice foodies. The city offers a varied and pleasant gastronomic experience, with selections ranging from traditional Belgian cuisine and Flemish delicacies to international eating options. Here is a detailed look at Antwerp's gastronomic offerings:

Traditional Belgian Cuisine

Hearty dishes that honor the nation's illustrious culinary heritage are a delight for the senses in traditional Belgian cuisine. Try these traditional Belgian delicacies when visiting Antwerp:

1. Moules-frites: This iconic Belgian dish consists of mussels steamed in a broth of white wine, shallots, and herbs, served with crispy golden fries.

2. Stoofvlees: Stoofvlees, sometimes referred to as Flemish beef stew, is a hearty dish that frequently comes with frites and is made of tender beef that has been cooked in a rich beer-based sauce.

3. Waterzooi: A creamy fish or chicken stew made with vegetables, potatoes, and a velvety broth.

4. Carbonade Flamande: Similar to stoofvlees, this beef and onion stew is cooked with dark beer, resulting in a deep and robust flavor.

5. Belgian Endive Gratin: A popular side dish made with endives (witloof) wrapped in ham and covered with a creamy cheese sauce.

Flemish Specialties and Beer

Like the rest of Flanders, Antwerp is well known for its love of beer and has a selection of local brewers. Trappist ales, Abbey beers, and the famed Belgian Tripels and Dubbels are some well-liked Flemish beer varieties to sample.

Enjoy delectable Flemish cheeses like Brugge Blomme, Herve, and Passendale to go with the beer. These cheeses are frequently offered with a variety of artisan bread.

International Dining Options

Due to the city's diversified population, there are many different international dining alternatives. There are restaurants and eating establishments that may satisfy your cravings for Italian, Greek, Japanese, Middle Eastern, or Indian food.

Chinatown in Antwerp is particularly famous for its authentic Chinese and Asian restaurants, where you can savor delicious dim sum, noodles, and other delicacies.

Local Food Markets

The food markets in Antwerp are a veritable treasure trove of sensations for food lovers who appreciate discovering regional goods and specialties. The following are some of the must-visit food markets include:

1. Antwerp Central Market: The busy Antwerp Central Market, which lies in the heart of the city, sells a range of local specialties, handmade crafts, and fresh food.

2. Exotic Market (Exotische Markt): This bustling market, located close to Theaterplein, is open on Saturdays and features a large selection of international foods, spices, and products.

3. Vrijdagmarkt (Friday Market): This weekly market is the perfect place to sample fresh seafood, cheese, and other regional specialties.

Frites and Waffles

Without indulging in frites and waffles, a trip to Belgium, including Antwerp, is not complete. Belgian fries are typically offered with a variety of sauces, such as mayonnaise, ketchup, andalouse sauce, and samurai sauce, and are thicker than conventional fries.

Belgian waffles come in two flavors: Liege waffles, which are rich and chewy, and Brussels waffles, which are light and airy. They frequently have whipped cream, powdered sugar, various fruits, or chocolate on top.

The best places to purchase these cherished Belgian delicacies in Antwerp are from street vendors or speciality waffle shops.

Overall, the culinary scene in Antwerp offers a fascinating fusion of traditional Belgian meals, regional specialties, foreign flavors, and sweet delights. To really appreciate Antwerp's vast and varied culinary offerings, you must explore the city's food markets, try the local beers, and try frites and waffles.

CHAPTER EIGHT:
Shopping in Antwerp

With an intriguing variety of shopping opportunities to suit all likes and budgets, Antwerp is a shopper's paradise. The city has something for everyone, whether you're seeking for high-end clothing, distinctive shops, vintage finds, delicious chocolates, or treasured mementos. Here is a detailed guide to shopping in Antwerp:

Fashion and Design District

Antwerp is renowned as a fashion capital, and its Fashion and Design District, also known as the ModeNatie, is at the heart of this reputation. Located around the Nationalestraat and the surrounding area, this district is home to some of

Belgium's most prestigious fashion designers and boutiques.

The Fashion Museum (MoMu) is a centerpiece of the district, showcasing fashion exhibits and collections that highlight Antwerp's influence on the global fashion scene.

Along with up-and-coming designers showcasing their avant-garde works, you can discover the flagship stores of Belgian designers like Dries Van Noten, Ann Demeulemeester, and Walter Van Beirendonck here. The neighborhood is a must-visit location for fashion fans due to its vibrant atmosphere and cutting-edge designs.

Antwerp's Fashion Boutiques

Beyond the Fashion and Design District, Antwerp is awash in chic stores that may accommodate a range of tastes and price ranges. You may find a variety of independent boutiques, hip stores, and well-known worldwide brands in the areas surrounding Kammenstraat, Lombardenvest, and Huidevettersstraat.

In addition, there are several concept stores in Antwerp where you can find a carefully curated assortment of clothes, accessories, and lifestyle items from well-known and up-and-coming designers.

Antiques and Vintage Shops

Antwerp is a treasure trove of one-of-a-kind finds for those who enjoy vintage and antique items. With multiple stores offering a diverse selection of antique furniture, home goods, works of art, and collectibles from various eras, Kloosterstraat is the go-to place for antiques.

For vintage shopping, the surrounding Hoogstraat and Kloosterstraat neighborhoods are also fantastic. In these vintage stores, you can get impressive retro clothing, unique accessories, and other items.

Souvenirs and Gifts

There are many options available if you're seeking for gifts and souvenirs to keep as a reminder of your vacation to Antwerp. There are many gift stores offering keychains, postcards, and trinkets in the city's major squares and sites. Visit specialist shops that sell handcrafted goods, such as crafts, art, and products from the area if you're looking for more original and genuine presents.

An excellent spot to discover gift and souvenir shops with a large assortment of items is Steenstraat, which is close to Steen Castle.

Chocolate and Confectionery

With its delicious chocolate stores, Antwerp proudly contributes to Belgium's famed chocolate industry. Find artisan chocolatiers throughout the city that offer a delectable selection of pralines, truffles, and chocolate bars.

There are numerous chocolate stores throughout the city center, especially in the Grote Markt and Meir districts, where you may indulge in the sweet treats of Belgian chocolate.

Shopping Tips in Antwerp

1. VAT Refund: If you don't live in the EU, you might be able to get your VAT back on your purchases. Look for stores bearing the "Tax Free Shopping" label, and ask the salesperson about the procedure.

2. Shop Opening Hours: The majority of Antwerp's stores open at 10:00 AM and close at 6:00 PM. Some stores may only be open for a short time or not at all on Sundays.

3. Payment Options: Credit cards are generally accepted in Antwerp, but it's a good idea to have some cash on hand in case you need to make a minor purchase or visit a place that only accepts cash.

4. Sale Periods: Visit during the official sales times, which normally take place between January and July, if you're seeking for savings.

5. Window Shopping: Don't forget to take advantage of window shopping, particularly in the fashion areas. Shop displays in Antwerp frequently feature imaginative design that is fascinating to look at.

6. Try Local Specialties: Don't be afraid to explore other local products, such as Belgian

beer, waffles, and speculoos (spiced biscuits), in addition to clothing and chocolates.

The varied shopping options in Antwerp invite you to discover their distinctive offers and bring home trinkets that capture the spirit and character of the city. Whether you're an art enthusiast, a fashionista, or a foodie, this energetic and vibrant Belgian city has numerous delights to offer.

CHAPTER NINE:
Nightlife in Antwerp

The nightlife in Antwerp is as vibrant and diversified as the city itself. Every taste and mood may be satisfied, from crowded bars and hip nightclubs to cozy jazz clubs and cultural events. Here's a detailed look at Antwerp's thriving nightlife scene:

Bars and Pubs

In Antwerp, there are many bars and pubs where locals and visitors congregate to mingle, unwind, and consume a variety of alcoholic beverages. Some of the most well-liked bar locations are:

1. Grote Markt: With a large number of bars and cafes, Antwerp's main square, Grote Markt, is a

bustling gathering place. The lovely location of the square is ideal for having a drink and people-watching.

2. Groenplaats: Groenplaats is a bustling square with bars and terraces close to the Cathedral of Our Lady that makes for a wonderful setting for a leisurely evening.

3. Zuid (South Antwerp): South Antwerp's trendy Zuid district is noted for its chic nightlife establishments and contemporary bars, which draw a young, fashionable audience.

4. Eilandje: The Eilandje neighborhood has experienced major redevelopment and is now home to fashionable bars with contemporary and modern surroundings near the river.

Trendy Nightclubs

Antwerp has a variety of hip nightclubs that can accommodate a variety of musical interests for those wishing to dance the night away. Some popular nightclubs include:

1. Club Vaag: Known for its techno and electronic music, Club Vaag is a favorite among electronic dance music enthusiasts.

2. Café d'Anvers: Since the late 1980s, Café d'Anvers has been a mainstay of Antwerp's nightlife and has been playing a mix of house and techno music.

3. Ampere: Ampere is a well-known club for fans of underground techno and electronic

music, and it features DJs from around the world.

Live Music Venues

In Antwerp, there are several live music venues that present performances in a wide range of musical genres. Top locations for live music include:

1. Trix: A multifaceted music venue that presents performances of rock, indie, hip-hop, and alternative music.

2. De Roma: A former theater that now serves as a concert venue, hosting a wide range of musical events.

3. Jazz Middelheim: Every year, the Middelheim Park hosts a jazz festival that attracts the best jazz performers from all over the world.

Jazz Bars and Cafés

For fans of jazz, Antwerp features a number of atmospheric jazz pubs and cafes that offer a welcoming environment to take in live jazz performances. Here are several jazz venues to check out:

1. Hopper: A hip jazz café well-known for its cozy ambiance and frequent jazz performances.

2. De Muze: This Antwerp institution for jazz has been a favorite hangout for fans since the 1960s.

Cultural Evenings

The cultural scene in Antwerp continues into the evenings and offers a variety of events and activities. There is always something going on in the city, from theatrical performances to poetry readings to art exhibitions.

Cultural performances and plays frequently take place at theaters like the Bourla Theatre and Antwerp Royal Theatre (Koninklijk Museum voor Schone Kunsten Antwerpen). Cultural institutions and art galleries may also host special events or openings in the evenings.

The nightlife in Antwerp is active and varied, catering to a variety of tastes and interests. The city boasts a vibrant nightlife culture that guarantees you have a wonderful and memorable time, whether you prefer dancing at hip nightclubs, listening to live music in welcoming places, or immersing yourself in cultural events.

CHAPTER TEN:
Outdoor Adventures near Antwerp

In addition to being a bustling metropolis, Antwerp serves as a starting point for a wealth of outdoor activities and scenic drives. There are many possibilities to enjoy nature and explore the area, from tranquil parks and natural spaces to picturesque bicycle routes and boat cruises. Here is a detailed look at outdoor activities close to Antwerp:

Parks and Green Spaces

1. Rivierenhof: Just outside of Antwerp's city limits, this sizable public park provides a tranquil escape from the hustle and bustle of the city. The park is ideal for leisurely walks, picnics, and outdoor activities because it has

lovely lakes, meadows, and wooded regions. Children's playgrounds and a number of inviting cafés are also present.

2. Park Spoor Noord is a well-liked destination for both locals and tourists. Large open areas, gardens, play areas, and a skate park are all present. Throughout the year, Park Spoor Noord holds a variety of events and festivals that foster a lively and welcoming environment.

3. Middelheim Park: As previously mentioned, Middelheim Park is not only a lovely sculpture park but also an art museum. The expansive, lush lawns and striking sculptures offer a singular mix of art and nature, fostering a meditative atmosphere.

Cycling and Biking Routes

1. Antwerp Port Cycling Route: Cycling through the Port of Antwerp, one of Europe's biggest and most important ports, is part of this route if you're interested in learning more about the city's nautical history. While cycling along the waterfront, take in the beautiful views of the river and dockyards.

2. Scheldt River Cycling Route: Cycling along the Scheldt River provides stunning views of the surrounding scenery and the river itself. Along the river's flow, the path passes through quaint towns, wilderness areas, and historic places.

3. Kalmthoutse Heide National Park: Kalmthoutse Heide National Park is a sizable nature reserve that is immediately north of

Antwerp and is renowned for its heathlands, sand dunes, and pine trees. With numerous clearly delineated paths that wind through the breathtaking natural surroundings, it's a great place for riding.

Boat Tours and Cruises

1. River Scheldt Boat Tours: A number of Antwerp businesses provide boat trips along the River Scheldt, offering distinctive views of the city's cityscape and waterfront. These excursions frequently include enlightening comments about Antwerp's past and famous sites.

2. Antwerp Canal Cruises: With guided canal cruises that travel past quaint communities and historic places, you can discover the city's picturesque waterways. An enjoyable and

picturesque approach to find Antwerp's hidden beauties is through canal cruises.

Day Trips to Surrounding Towns

1. Ghent: Approximately an hour's drive from Antwerp, Ghent is a charming city with a rich medieval history. Its picturesque canals, historical architecture, and vibrant atmosphere make it a perfect destination for a day trip.

2. Bruges: Known as the "Venice of the North," Bruges is a city on the UNESCO World Heritage List that is well-known for its picturesque canals and well-preserved medieval buildings. A day trip to Bruges gives visitors the chance to stroll through its cobblestone streets, see important historical sites, and savor delectable Belgian chocolates.

3. Mechelen: The St. Rumbold's Cathedral and the Mechelen Toy Museum are just two of the many cultural attractions in this quaint town, which is not far from Antwerp.

Sports and Recreation

1. Watersport Center De Nekker: Located in Mechelen, a short drive from Antwerp, De Nekker provides a variety of water-based sports like kayaking, paddleboarding, and swimming in the outdoor pool.

2. Antwerpse Kempen: To the east of Antwerp, the Antwerpse Kempen region provides many chances for outdoor activities and recreation, such as horseback riding, hiking, and mountain biking through beautiful forests and heathlands.

3. Golf Courses: There are a number of golf courses in and near Antwerp that allow players to tee off amid picturesque scenery and lush greens.

Antwerp and its environs provide a wealth of outdoor activities for everyone to enjoy, whether you like peaceful strolls in the park, cycling through picturesque landscapes, seeing neighboring towns, or taking part in numerous sports and activities.

CHAPTER ELEVEN:
Unraveling Antwerp's History

The strategic position, economic strength, and cultural accomplishments of Antwerp have produced its rich and varied history. The history of the city is a tapestry of amazing tales, from its Golden Age as a vibrant commercial and artistic center to its lasting legacy in the diamond trade and the effects of World War II on its landscape. Here is a detailed look at the fascinating history of Antwerp:

Antwerp's Golden Age

During the 16th century, when it rose to become one of Europe's most important and rich cities, Antwerp experienced its Golden Age. As a significant port and trading hub, Antwerp experienced a boom in global trade, particularly in the markets for wool, cloth, and luxury products.

The city's advantageous location on the River Scheldt drew traders from all over Europe, and its stock exchange eventually became the first recognized stock market in the world. Antwerp was a melting pot of cultures that drew intellectuals, artists, and professors from all over the world, creating a vibrant arts and cultural scene.

During this time, Flemish artists like Peter Paul Rubens and Anthony van Dyck gained notoriety and created works of art that established Antwerp as a major hub for the arts. The city still boasts magnificent structures, cathedrals, and art collections that serve as reminders of this Golden Age.

The Diamond Trade Legacy

Antwerp became the center of the diamond industry in the 19th century. The city's diamond quarter developed into a major trading and cutting hub for diamonds, where talented artisans produced priceless jewelry and precious stones.

When Antwerp founded the Diamond High Council, a body that oversees the diamond business and assures ethical procedures, the city cemented its legacy in the diamond trade. Antwerp continues to be one of the most significant diamond trading hubs in the world today, playing a significant part in the diamond supply chain.

World War II and Its Impact

Due to its strategic significance as a vital port, Antwerp faced severe difficulties and sustained significant damage during World War II. German forces were in control of the city, and Allied bombing raids frequently targeted its port.

When the Allies effectively rid the Scheldt estuary of German defenses during the Battle of the Scheldt in 1944, the port of Antwerp was able to reopen and receive important supplies. This triumph was crucial to the liberation of northern France and Belgium.

Even though the city's historic core was mostly rebuilt after the war, the city's architecture and monuments nevertheless contain remnants of the past.

Architectural Heritage

The city of Antwerp has a rich architectural history that reflects its historical and cultural importance. The city features a stunning fusion of Gothic, Renaissance, Baroque, and Art Nouveau architecture.

The Antwerp Central Station, designed by architect Louis Delacenserie, is an exquisite example of railway architecture and is often referred to as one of the most beautiful train stations in the world.

One of the most stunning train stations in the world is the Louis Delacenserie-designed Antwerp Central Station, which is a stunning example of railway architecture.

Art and Cultural Heritage

With a history of cultivating artistic expression and creating significant artists, Antwerp has a strong artistic heritage. The city's art museums, including the Museum aan de Stroom (MAS) and the Royal Museum of Fine Arts (KMSKA), have significant collections that cover centuries of artistic accomplishments.

Flemish masters like Anthony van Dyck and Peter Paul Rubens left a lasting impression on the city's cultural legacy, and their works are honored and displayed in numerous museums and historic structures.

With bustling theaters, galleries, and music venues that highlight the city's innovative character and unwavering commitment for the arts, Antwerp is still today a dynamic cultural hub.

From its Golden Age as a thriving commercial and cultural powerhouse to its current status as a dynamic and culturally rich city, unraveling Antwerp's past offers an engrossing voyage through time. Travelers seeking a fusion of history, culture, and artistic magnificence will find Antwerp to be a compelling destination thanks to its architectural marvels, artistic heritage, and global prominence in the diamond trade.

CHAPTER TWELVE:
Insider's Tips for a Memorable Antwerp Vacation

With its fascinating history, active cultural scene, and welcoming residents, Antwerp makes for a wonderful vacation destination. Here are some insider recommendations to make the most of your trip and fully experience the charm of the city:

Local Etiquette and Customs

1. Greetings: When meeting locals, a handshake is the standard form of greeting. In more informal settings, like a social gathering with friends, a kiss on the cheek is common as a friendly gesture.

2. Language: Although Dutch (Flemish) is the dominant language in Antwerp, you'll discover that many residents are equally fluent in English. The locals can appreciate learning a few fundamental Dutch expressions like "dank u" (thank you) and "goedemorgen" (good morning).

3. Tipping: In Antwerp, leaving a tip is not required because most restaurants already include service fees in their prices. However, it is considered courteous to give a little tip for good service. It's customary to round up the total or leave a 5–10% tip.

4. Cycling Etiquette: Using hand signals to indicate turns and yielding to pedestrians on shared pathways are just a few examples of proper cycling etiquette. If you decide to ride around the city, keep these regulations in mind.

Money-Saving Tips

1. Antwerp City Card: Consider obtaining an Antwerp municipal Card, which entitles you to free entry to a variety of museums, attractions, and municipal transportation. Additionally, it offers discounts at numerous eateries and stores.

2. Picnics in the Parks: Antwerp has lovely parks where you may take a leisurely picnic. Shop at local farmers' markets for fresh products, then relax with a wallet-friendly supper amidst a lush setting.

3. Pre-book Attractions: Many popular attractions offer discounts for online bookings or combo tickets. Plan ahead and save money by purchasing tickets in advance.

4. Happy Hours: Take advantage of happy hours at bars and pubs, usually held in the early evening, for discounted drinks and snacks.

Off-the-Beaten-Path Spots

1. Het Eilandje Marina: Explore the Het Eilandje district, which is less touristy but offers a charming marina, beautiful waterfront views, and trendy bars and restaurants.

2. St. Paul's Church: While the Cathedral of Our Lady is a must-see, St. Paul's Church is worth checking out for its gorgeous Baroque interior and serene atmosphere.

3. Vrijdagmarkt: On a Friday morning, go to Vrijdagmarkt to see a local flea market where

you may find antiques, used goods, and one-of-a-kind products.

4. Red Star Line Museum: At this less well-known but interesting museum, learn about the experiences of immigrants who sailed from Antwerp to the United States in the late 19th and early 20th centuries.

Safety Precautions

1. Pickpocketing: Be on the lookout for pickpockets in busy places and on public transit, as you would in any tourist destination. Keep your possessions safe, and don't show off any pricey goods.

2. Street Safety: Although Antwerp is often safe, it's important to remain alert, especially at night.

Avoid dimly lit or empty streets and stay in well-lit, crowded places.

3. Public Transportation: The city of Antwerp has dependable and safe public transit. However, while riding trams and buses, especially during rush hour, keep an eye on your stuff.

4. Emergency Numbers: Familiarize yourself with the local emergency numbers, such as 112 for general emergencies and 101 for police assistance.

You can have a truly memorable and enriching holiday in Antwerp by embracing local culture, being frugal with your money, seeing off-the-beaten-path locations, and being careful with safety precautions. Make the most of the city's rich culture, history, and welcoming people to make your trip one to remember.

CHAPTER THIRTEEN: Appendix

30 Useful Phrases in Dutch and Pronunciation Guide

Here are some useful phrases in Dutch to help you communicate during your visit to Antwerp:

1. Hello - Hallo (hah-loh)
2. Good morning - Goedemorgen (khoo-duh-mor-khuhn)
3. Good afternoon - Goedemiddag (khoo-duh-mi-dahkh)
4. Good evening - Goedenavond (khoo-duh-nah-vohnt)
5. Goodbye - Tot ziens (tot zeens)
6. Please - Alstublieft (ahl-stoo-bleeft)
7. Thank you - Dank u (dahnk uu)

8. Yes - Ja (yah)

9. No - Nee (nay)

10. Excuse me - Excuseer mij (eks-koo-zeer may)

11. Sorry - Sorry (sor-ee)

12. I don't understand - Ik begrijp het niet (ik buh-grayp hut neet)

13. Can you help me? - Kunt u mij helpen? (kunt uu may help-uhn?)

14. Where is...? - Waar is...? (var is...?)

15. How much is this? - Hoeveel kost dit? (hoo-veyl kost dit?)

16. I would like... - Ik zou graag... (ik zow graakh...)

17. What time is it? - Hoe laat is het? (hoo laat is hut?)

18. Cheers! - Proost! (prohst!)

19. Do you speak English? - Spreekt u Engels? (spreekt uu enguls?)

20. My name is... - Mijn naam is... (main naam is...)

21. Where is the bathroom? - Waar is het toilet? (var is hut twah-let?)

22. Can I have the bill? - Mag ik de rekening? (mahkh ik duh ray-nink?)

23. Help! - Help! (help!)

24. I'm lost - Ik ben verdwaald (ik ben vuhr-dwahlt)

25. Is there a pharmacy nearby? - Is er een apotheek in de buurt? (is uhr un ah-pohek in duh buhrt?)

26. I love Antwerp - Ik hou van Antwerpen (ik how vahn ahnt-vur-puhn)

27. What is your name? - Hoe heet u? (hoo hate uu?)

28. Can you recommend a good restaurant? - Kunt u een goed restaurant aanbevelen? (kunt uu un khoot rest-oh-rant ahn-buh-vuh-luhn?)

29. Where can I buy souvenirs? - Waar kan ik souvenirs kopen? (var kahn ik sou-vuh-neers koh-puhn?)

30. Have a nice day! - Een fijne dag! (uhn fay-nuh dahkh!)

Note: The pronunciation guide provides approximate phonetic pronunciations to help with speaking Dutch. However, for more accurate pronunciation, consider using language learning resources or consulting a native speaker.

Currency Conversion Chart

As currency exchange rates fluctuate, it's best to check real-time rates on reliable financial websites or apps. However, here are some rough conversions to give you an idea:

- 1 Euro (EUR) ≈ 1.12 US Dollar (USD)

- 1 Euro (EUR) ≈ 0.85 British Pound (GBP)
- 1 Euro (EUR) ≈ 1.48 Canadian Dollar (CAD)
- 1 Euro (EUR) ≈ 1.58 Australian Dollar (AUD)
- 1 Euro (EUR) ≈ 129 Japanese Yen (JPY)
- 1 Euro (EUR) ≈ 8.52 Chinese Yuan (CNY)

Please note that exchange rates can vary depending on where you exchange your money, so it's best to compare rates and consider fees before making currency conversions.

Packing List for Antwerp

When packing for your trip to Antwerp, consider the season and the activities you plan to enjoy. Here's a comprehensive packing list to get you started:

- Clothing:

- Weather-appropriate clothing (layers for varying temperatures)
- Comfortable walking shoes
- Raincoat or umbrella (especially in the rainy season)
- Swimsuit (if visiting during summer)

- Travel Essentials:
- Passport and travel documents
- Travel insurance details
- Local currency or credit/debit cards
- Power adapter and chargers for electronic devices
- Personal medication and first-aid kit

- Personal Items:
- Sunscreen and sunglasses
- Hat or cap for sun protection
- Toiletries (toothbrush, toothpaste, etc.)

- Hand sanitizer and wet wipes

- Camera or smartphone for capturing memories

- Miscellaneous:

- Guidebook or map of Antwerp
- Reusable water bottle
- Day bag or backpack for excursions
- Snacks for on-the-go

By considering the local customs, converting your currency, packing wisely, and ensuring your safety, you can have a memorable and enjoyable vacation in Antwerp. Remember to immerse yourself in the city's culture, explore its hidden gems, and make the most of your time in this vibrant and historic Belgian city.

MAP OF ANTWERP

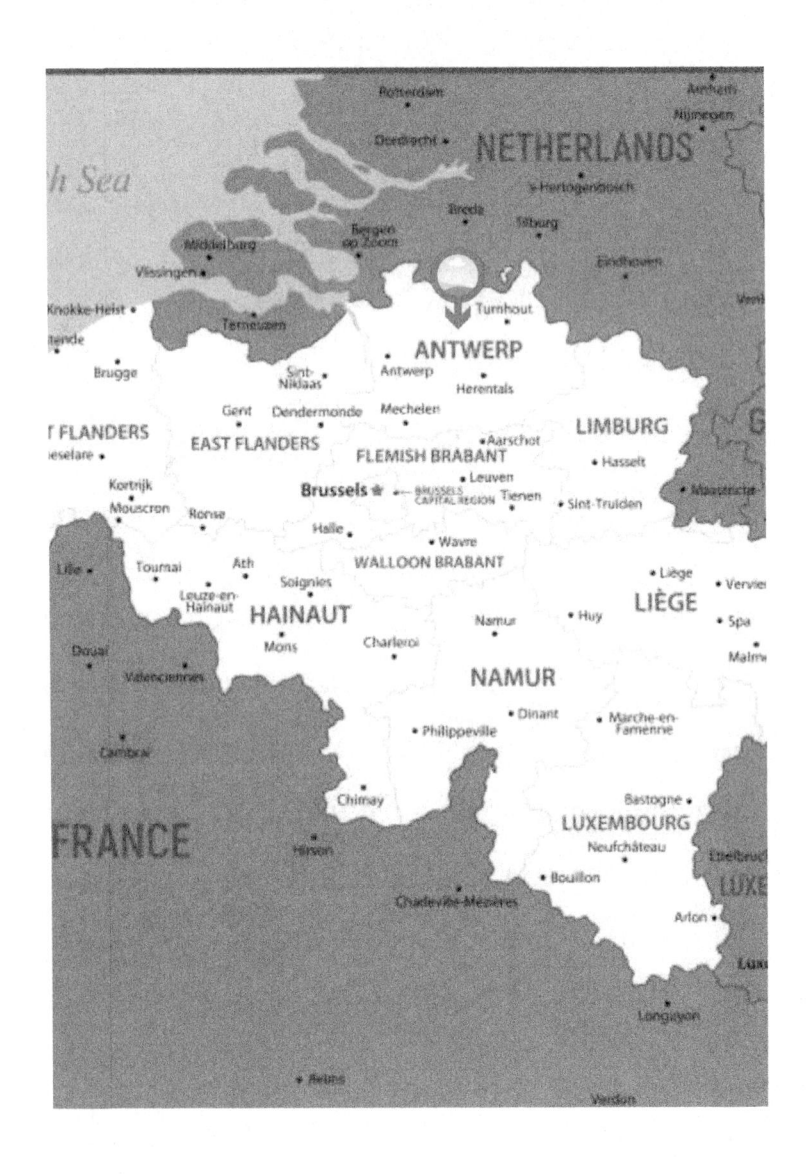

Printed in Great Britain
by Amazon